Christmas Poems

For Children

George Stanworth

Illustrated by Matthew L

ISBN:1539323463

ISBN-13:978-1539323464

DEDICATIONS

For my daughter, Cadence Stanworth, and for my step-son, Michael
Hastings.

Love you both very much xx

CONTENTS

SANTA

S anta slipped on Rudolph's smelly socks

A nd underpants,

N early falling down the

T oilet.

A reindeer laughed, and Santa laughed back too.

CHRISTMAS IS NEARING AGAIN

When the air starts to turn,

and the coal fires burn

then Christmas is nearing again.

When the children that play

start to warm up the day

then Christmas is nearing again.

When the elves start to fly

through the Wedding dress sky

then Christmas is nearing again.

When the beautiful sounds

of carols abound

then Christmas is nearing again.

When the trees look divine

in their tinsel design,

then Christmas is nearing again

When Santa has done

his final test run

then Christmas is nearing again.

THE ADVENT CALENDAR

1 What	2 picture	3 does	4 the
5 window	6 hide?	7 It	8 comes
9 as	10 a	11 surprise.	12 I
13 love	14 to	15 guess	16 what's
17 coming	18 next,	19 but	20 always
21 love	22 the	23 chocolate	24 best!

I LOVE YOU MUM

Mum, you are my candlelight,

my angel, and my Silent Night.

More precious than a gift of gold

who wraps me up when I am cold.

Mum, you are my Christmas Day,

my North Star, and my snow bouquet.

You are my joy, my verse, my rhyme,

who I love more each Christmas time.

IF CHRISTMAS WAS A SPACESHIP

If Christmas was a lesson,

I'd say 'Hip hip hooray!'

and tell all of my teachers

to teach it every day.

If Christmas was a vegetable,

I'd eat it up for sure;

and tell my Mum and Dad each meal

to give me so much more.

If Christmas was my sister,

I'd always treat her right,

and never want to push her,

or tease to start a fight.

If Christmas was a Spaceship,

I'd always want to go

to visit boring relatives

whose names I never know.

If Christmas was forever,

(which I believe it should),

then I would never misbehave –

and promise to be good.

BRR! BRR! BRR!

Brr! Brr! Brr!

Myrrh! Myrrh! Myrrh!

Gold! Gold! Gold!

Cold! Cold! Cold!

Snow! Snow! Snow!

Ho! Ho! Ho!

Sleigh! Sleigh! Sleigh!

Play! Play! Play!

Tree! Tree! Tree!

Whee! Whee! Whee!

Snow! Snow! Snow!

Ho! Ho! Ho!

THE CHRISTMAS WISH LIST

"I don't think that I need that much,
this Christmas - just a rabbit hutch,
and maybe rabbits, plus a dog,
a guinea-pig, and rainbow frog.

I'd like some books on Mickey Mouse,
a tractor, and a large tree-house.
I'd like some shoes. I'd like a coat.
I'd love a real size pirate boat.

I'd like some swings. I'd like a slide.
I'd like to have a bike to ride.
I'd love some drums to bash and hit;
an aeroplane, a big spaceship.

I'd like an I-Pad, like a horse,

love a swimming pool of course.

I'd like a beach. I'd like a town.

I'd love the world. Don't turn me down!

Santa, see, I don't need much.

I never like to cause a fuss,

but if there's more that I remember,

I'll write again before December!

I WANT A SLEDGE WITH WINGS ON

I want a sledge

with wings on,

like an aeroplane,

so I can soar above the snow clouds,

and fight the sky monster

to save the snowflake crowds;

Then once the monster fled

I want a sledge

with a super-sonic jet engine

so I can zoom past all my friends

and lift a trophy with both hands,

and send a text from foreign lands,

then when I'm bored with being so ahead;

I think instead

I'd want a sledge

with built-in Christmas dinner,

and Christmas pudding on the side,

with roasted chestnuts, Yuletide log,

and fizzy drinks - I'd have the lot!

A Christmas feast. I'd never stop

until I'm just about to pop,

and then I think I'd go and hop

into my snug and cosy bed.

MISLED

There wasn't snow last winter.

I felt I'd been misled.

I couldn't throw a snowball,

so threw some sprouts instead!

ANTICIPATION

Waiting for winter

in darkening nights.

Waiting to set up

the tree and the lights.

Waiting to write the

cards I will send.

Waiting, just waiting

for school-term to end.

Waiting to sledge.

Waiting for snow.

Waiting at Grotto's

is always so slow.

Waiting for bedtime

in thimble like noise.

Waiting for Santa.

waiting for toys.

The waiting is over.

It's Christmas at last.

Waiting no more

for the time to go fast.

Christmas is over.

I wish it could stay.

Now I start waiting

for next Christmas Day!

BIG EARS DAD

My Dad has very big ears
as he always hears me say
'Bogey' even when I whisper it
under my breath.

He hates me saying 'Bogey'
but sometimes I forget,
which makes him quite upset
and ends up with me on the naughty step.

He tells me Santa does not like naughty children
and may not come,
but saying 'Bogey' makes me laugh -
yet not as much as saying 'Bum!'

THE TWELVE DAYS OF CHRISTMAS

12. When

11. Asked

10. For

9. My

8. Favourite

7. Day

6. Of

5. Christmas,

4. I

3. Replied

2. Back

1. 'All of them'

WHEEEEEEEEEEEEEEE!

My happy tummy and frozen bogeys await;
  await their fate, at the back of the giggling line,
    on the peak of the cold divine
      hill that discards clouds like hats.

n

        Scarves are wrapped to keep out cold,
          and keep in fear, so everyone when time is near
            can cheer and make out all is fine.
i
            My time has come.
            My face is numb. I S
a   L
                           I
                            D
                             E
                        and hide
g   my doubts
                       behind my eyes.
 a   W
                              H
   and   E
                              E!
        It's glee. It's 'Yeah,yeah,yeah' and just don't care.
  n
                              R I
  i   C K
                      E T
  a   Y
  g   BUMP! I
                              S
  a   L
                             ump
  and   and thump my knee.
        I'm in pain, but I'll keep on sledging a g a in and
    n   a
         i   a   g

24

LIFE IS TOUGH WHEN YOU'RE FOUR AND A HALF

Writing to Santa, eating mince pies,

staring at snow that falls from the sky;

Jumping on sofas, writing some cards,

life is tough when you're four and a half.

Singing some carols, having a sneeze,

helping put baubles and stars on the trees;

Talking to snowmen, having a laugh,

life is tough when you're four and a half.

Painting a reindeer, making a mess,

getting your stocking, feeling the best;

Falling to sleep after Christmas Eve bath,

as life is tough when you're four and a half!

SNOW!

Snow that falls down from the roofs,

Snow that's found on Rudolph's hooves,

Snow as cold as Santa's breath,

Snow as warm as Robin's breast.

Snow that's light, and snow to throw,

Snow that's fast and snow that's slow.

Snow that's icy, snow that thaws,

Snow that makes you want to pause.

Snow from a romantic scene,

Snow that's like the perfect dream.

Snow that's pretty. Snow that's rough.

Tired snow that's had enough.

Snow of beauty. Snow unique.

Snow that makes my world complete.

NOT ME DAD!

IT
WAS   NOT   ME

THAT   KNOCKED   OVER
THE   CHRISTMAS   TREE.

IT   WAS   THE
ANGEL,   OR   MAYBE

IT   WAS   A
BUMBLE -   BEE.   TRUTH -

FUL -   LY   IT
WAS   NOT

ME!

FALLING

```
S   F   F   T   S   A   D   T   C
N   A   A   H   A   B   O   H   H
O   L   S   A   N   S   W   E   I
W   L   T   N   T   E   N       M
    S   E       A   I           N
        R           L           E
                    I           Y
                    N
                    G
```

WHEN I GET OLDER

When I get older, I want to apply
to do Santa's job, and fly in the sky
with Rudolph and Blitzen and all of the others,
viewing the roofs tablecloth covered.

Going down chimneys, not making a peep,
laying down presents near children asleep.
Flying back happy with joy all the way
knowing that children have had a great day.

THE DAY THAT CHRISTMAS CAME

The day that Christmas came,

presents were stacked.

Trees were up.

Christmas is a delight.

(by Cadence Stanworth aged 5)

THE SNOW KNIGHT

A dragon

built a 'Snow Knight'

so it could have a fight,

but sneezed and blew out fire

that set the knight alight.

The 'Snow Knight' quickly melted.

The dragon shed a tear.

'I didn't mean to hurt him,

just make him feel some fear.'

'I know you didn't mean it.'

I told him. 'Don't you cry.

You can always build another

after eating 'Ice-Cream Pie.'

That way, you won't breathe fire,

but ice, which should be fine,

then you can fight the 'Snow-Knight'

and have a roaring time.'

YOU CAN'T BUILD A ROAD WHILE I'M EATING CHRISTMAS DINNER!

While having a great Christmas time,

a thing occurred of the sublime.

An animated lorry-load

of dolls started to build a road.

'Excuse me Maam', I said aloud.

'I'm sure that this is not allowed'.

She disagreed, and before my eye,

took a bite of my mince pie.

She said the work had been approved,

so asked why I had not yet moved.

I said I'd not been told before.

Her teeny weeny voice laughed 'Sure'.

Angels drove some JCBs,

whilst snowmen got down on their knees,

and marked some spots with lots of crosses

(I hoped I was insured for losses.)

I pleaded 'Stop! You've got to cease,

unless I'll have to call the police.

A fairy in a Policeman's hat

said 'We'll have to have no more of that'.

There's hundreds coming here tonight

for switching on of traffic lights.

Move your sofas, stop your moans.

We've got to put down traffic cones'.

They dug up carpets, painted lines,

and gave me their first traffic fine.

A year ago was this event,

and I'm still eating fried cement!

So be alert, and be aware,

(although this type of thing is rare).

Don't be caught by this new crime,

unless a road you'll have this Christmas time!

WHOOPS!

My Dad slipped on a bauble.

My Mum was in a state.

Dad fell on the table

and squashed the Christmas Cake!

A WEE MELTDOWN

The wet patch in our

hall was the snowman who failed

to reach the toilet.

AN ALIEN TOOK MY CHRISTMAS TREE

An alien took my Christmas tree

and wouldn't give it back.

I told him that was naughty,

but he put it in a sack.

I chased him through the garden.

I chased him through the park.

I chased him in the daylight.

I chased him in the dark.

He ran towards a doorway

with lots of flashing lights.

I didn't want to follow

as it wasn't safe or right.

It may have been a spaceship,

and then I would be trapped,

taken into outer space,

and never coming back.

There could be slimy creatures

whose manner wasn't mild.

There could be one eyed monsters

who want to eat a child.

I started walking home again,

feeling quite deflated;

but then I heard a roar behind,

which made me feel elated.

My friends were there all laughing

at my brother's great disguise,

and shouted 'It's your party.

It's your Christmas Eve surprise!'

IT'S CHRISTMAS EVE ALREADY

"It's Christmas Eve already.

I really cannot wait.

I'm bouncing with excitement,

tomorrow will be great.

It's Christmas Eve already.

I need to get to sleep,

so Santa brings me presents

that I can always keep.

It's Christmas Eve already.

I can't believe it's true."

"But Gran, you'll find that Santa

will visit me, not you!"

EXCITEMENT BUILDS

Excitement

builds,   like

a snowman   waiting

for   his   jacket,   scarf,

hat, pipe, body and head.

I BUILT A ROBOT SANTA

I built a robot fairytale,

and filled it up with smiles,

then asked it nicely if it could

spread its love for miles.

I built a robot song machine

precisely as I should,

and asked it to sing carols to

everyone it could.

I built a robot snowman.

The best one that I've done.

I told it to throw snowballs

at every Dad and Mum.

I built a robot Rudolph
inside the lavatory,
then told it 'I'm its master,
and it must follow me.'

I built a robot Santa
and gave it a large sack,
then ordered it to Lapland
to bring me presents back.

.

I planned to build a robot
to meet my final goal
of taking over every school
through magic mind control.

The teachers heard a whisper though

and said that I would pay,

but then I built a robot

that took them far away.

The police were not that happy

and said it was a crime,

so I travelled in a time machine

to 1989.

A CHRISTMAS MESSAGE

Christmas should be caring,

not focusing on greed.

Christmas is community

and helping those in need.

I PULLED THE CRACKER FAR TOO FAST

I pulled the cracker far too fast,

and knocked poor Grandma off her seat.

Mum and Dad were both aghast.

I pulled the cracker far too fast,

and Grandpa moaned about the 'blast'

which made him sneeze upon the meat.

I pulled the cracker far too fast,

and knocked poor Grandma off her seat.

I JUMPED INTO A CHRISTMAS CARD

I jumped into a Christmas card
and knocked off Santa's beard.
Rudolph was upset with me,
and all the snowmen jeered.

I said it was an accident,
but I would right the wrong.
I'd go and get some Sellotape
to stick the beard back on.

The elves said they would fix it,
but I could still assist
helping fight the monster
with the giant hands and wrists.

"This monster likes to pick us up,

and move us" said the elves.

"We end up in a shopfront,

on the walls, or on the shelves."

I said that's not a monster,

It's a human just like me.

The elves became hysterical

and screamed "We have to flee!"

I said I was a nice guy,

and wouldn't hurt a flea.

I'd only come to visit

as your world seemed cool to me.

They soon began to trust me,

and slowly stopped their sobbing,

then whistled to the snowman,

and the Christmas tree and robin.

We held a party in the snow,

and had a merry ball,

then sang a song entitled-

'Merry Christmas one and all.'

OTHER BOOKS FROM GEORGE

George Stanworth was born in Shropshire in England and has performed at numerous schools, libraries, community centres and entertainment facilities across the UK.

George's other publications include:-

Don't Trick Or Treat A Lion (3-8 Year Olds)
Moo Moo The Doodle (2-5 Year Olds)
Summer Poems For Kids (5-10 Year Olds))

Short Funny Love Poems
Snooker Poems
Darts Poems
Summer Poems For Kids

All of the above books can be purchased on Amazon:-

www.georgestanworth.co.uk

Printed in Great Britain
by Amazon

50616308R00029